WOMEN OF
VALOR

Other books in the REAL LIVES series

WOMEN OF
VALOR

edited by
Miriam Rinn

Cover illustration by Frank Morris

Copyright © 1999 by Troll Communications L.L.C.

Printed in the United States of America.   ISBN 0-8167-4931-0

10 9 8 7 6 5 4 3 2 1

TABLE OF CONTENTS

Sacajawea

Sacajawea raced her brother Cameahwait across the flat plain in front of the long row of tepees. "Faster, Arrow, faster!" she cried to her horse.

"Move, Eagle!" Cameahwait shouted. "Don't let her catch us!"

They rode for a mile. Sometimes Sacajawea darted ahead of her brother. Then his horse charged into the lead. They were both fast riders. They had the swiftest horses because their father was Chief of the Shoshone tribe.

All Shoshone braves knew how to ride. They had to move quickly to hunt the buffalo. Once a year, the Shoshones raced down from the Rocky Mountains to hunt, and since they had no guns, they had to move fast. Down on the plains, enemy Indians had guns and wanted fine Shoshone horses.

Not every Shoshone girl could ride, and none could ride as swiftly as Sacajawea. Today she and her brother were having fun, but tomorrow, Cameahwait would ride in the hunt with the other braves. The people needed the buffalo's meat and hide. Without the buffalo, they would be hungry and cold all winter.

Sacajawea and her brother rode like the wind. Suddenly, the

air was filled with the crack of gunfire. Sacajawea's horse reared up, throwing her to the ground.

"Little sister!" Cameahwait cried out. Sacajawea did not answer. Cameahwait was frightened. Hearing his father's loud war cry, he raced into the battle.

Soon it was done. The Shoshone Chief fell, and many braves died with him that day. The rest of the Shoshones raced back to the mountains. When Cameahwait reached the high ground, he looked down to where the camp had been. Smoke filled the sky. The tepees were burning, and many horses had been stolen. Cameahwait felt he had lost everything. He had lost his father. He had even lost his little sister, Sacajawea. There was much sorrow.

But Sacajawea was not dead. During the battle, she had hidden behind the rocks at the river's edge. When she saw her father fall, she cried out. Shivering with fright, she screamed again as a tall Minnetaree warrior picked her up on his stolen horse. Quickly, he rode away from the smoking Shoshone camp.

For many days they traveled fast across the flat plains. Looking back, Sacajawea could not see the great mountains where her people lived. Her heart was filled with sadness. She was no longer a Shoshone princess. She was a slave.

Her new life was strange. Her own people had been wanderers, but now, from one moon to the next, she lived in one place. The Minnetaree houses were round mounds of earth, and when winter came, she was warmer than she had been in her father's tepee. Still, she was lonely. She was not as hungry as she had been in the mountains. With their guns, the Minnetarees could kill more buffalo. But Sacajawea often thought of her mother and sister as she sewed buffalo skins by the fire.

For three years she worked for the wives of the Minnetaree warriors. When spring came, she learned to plant corn. Working in the garden, she thought of the wild berries in the great mountains.

Then, one day, something happened that made her sure she would never see her people again.

"Sacajawea," said the Minnetaree warrior, "you have grown too old to stay with us. I have sold you to this man. You will be his wife."

Sacajawea said nothing.

"His name is Charbonneau. You will go with him."

Charbonneau was a trapper from Canada. Sacajawea did not know where his people lived, and she did not understand the words he spoke to other white men who traveled on the river. She hoped they would live as her people did, hunting and trapping, but Charbonneau took her to live near the Mandan Indians on the Missouri River.

It was as if she had never left the Minnetarees.

That fall, Sacajawea was gathering firewood in her little boat. As she paddled toward home, she heard beating tom-toms and loud shouting.

Sacajawea was frightened. What should she do? Was this another battle?

As she came around the bend, she saw three boats. On the largest one, a bright red, white, and blue banner was waving in the wind. Sacajawea could see many strangers. She had never seen so many white men before. From their boats the strangers brought gifts for the Indians.

Sacajawea watched as her husband talked first to the strangers and then to the Indians. She felt proud that they needed Charbonneau to understand each other.

"Who are these men?" the Mandan chief asked Charbonneau.

"They come from a tribe of white men." Charbonneau pointed to the east. "They come in peace. This is Captain William Clark." A tall red-haired man stepped forward. "He is one of their leaders." Charbonneau gestured toward another man. "This is Captain Meriwether Lewis, their other leader."

"What do they want here?" asked the Mandan Chief.

"They wish to stay here for the winter. They will build a fort. When spring comes, they will travel on." Charbonneau pointed to the west.

Sacajawea felt her heart beating like tom-toms.

All winter, many Indians talked with the Captains. The Indians told Lewis and Clark what they knew about the land and about the tribes they would meet in the West. Charbonneau helped them to understand the Indians' words.

One night Charbonneau told Sacajawea, "When spring comes, I will go with the Captains. They will cross the far mountains to reach the great water."

On a snowy day in February, Sacajawea's son was born. She called him Pomp. "It is the Shoshone word for 'first-born,'" Charbonneau told the Captains.

"Shoshone?" Captain Clark asked. "She is of the Shoshone people who live in the Rocky Mountains?"

Sacajawea smiled.

"She is Shoshone," said Charbonneau.

He had told Lewis and Clark about the Shoshone horses. The Captains knew they might need horses to cross the Rockies. "Does she remember the language of her people?" Clark asked. "Can she help us find their camp?"

Charbonneau did not need to ask Sacajawea. "You will come with us," he told her that night.

They sailed up the Missouri that April. Sacajawea sat in the first boat, with little Pomp on her back.

"Indians along the river will know we come in peace," Charbonneau told the Captains. "Indians do not take women and children into battle."

Sacajawea was happy to be a sign of peace, but she was even happier to be going home at last.

*   *   *

It was slow, hard work going up the river, and the travelers did not know that it would get harder and harder.

One day the Captains went ashore to hunt. They left Sacajawea and Pomp with Charbonneau and another man in one of the boats on the river. Suddenly, a great gust of wind whipped the boat sideways.

"Help!" Charbonneau screamed. "Help me! I cannot swim!"

"Sit down!" Captain Lewis yelled from the shore. "Sit down, man! You'll tip the boat over!"

"Cut the sail!" Captain Clark shouted. He was ready to jump into the river to help, but the men held him back.

The boat was swiftly filling with water. Charbonneau was so frightened that he was no help at all, but Sacajawea quickly grabbed many things that were starting to float away. She saved medicine, maps, and supplies that would be needed for the days ahead. At last the boat was safely on the river bank. Clark was so grateful to Sacajawea that he gave her a belt of blue beads.

For many days they traveled. After a while, they began to hear a sound like thunder. It was not thunder, but a huge waterfall! Sacajawea was happy. She had heard her people talk of the falling water. She knew she was getting closer to her home.

"We will have to go around the falls on land," Captain Lewis decided. For weeks the men worked hard to build wagons to carry the boats on land. They did not realize that their troubles were just beginning. It was not easy to get through the narrow canyons and up the steep, rocky hills. One day the sky seemed to open. Thunder boomed! Rain rushed down, filling the narrow canyon path where the travelers walked.

"Go up!" Captain Clark shouted. "You must climb higher up the canyon walls!"

"Oh! No!" Charbonneau screamed. He was so frightened he did not remember his wife and child.

"Higher!" Captain Clark yelled. "We must climb higher!"

"Pomp!" Sacajawea cried out as the child slid from her arms. Rocks slipped under her feet when she tried to catch him.

Captain Clark grabbed Pomp. "Keep going!" With Pomp under his arm, he helped Sacajawea and saved them both from drowning.

But their troubles were not yet over. Along the way there were rattlesnakes and grizzly bears. Rain and hail came, and it was so cold! The path was rough and muddy. Many in the group became sick. Sacajawea almost died.

Finally, the day came when everyone felt better. Soon they were able to put the boats into the river again. They journeyed for many long miles before they reached the place where the Missouri River splits into three big streams.

Captain Lewis looked at the three branches of water. Which way should he follow? "This way," he pointed. He named the river for his friend Thomas Jefferson, the president of the United States. Everyone prayed that they were headed in the right direction— toward the great water called the Pacific Ocean.

After many long days on the water, Sacajawea pointed to some round rocks on the shore. This was where she had tried to hide from the Minnetarees! "I have been here before!" she exclaimed. She held little Pomp close to her heart. So much had passed since that day. But where were her people?

Each day they looked for Shoshones.

"Here," Sacajawea said. "They have been here." She showed them smoking campfires along the river. She showed them footprints of Indian feet. But they saw no Indians.

"If we do not get horses, we will never make it over the mountains," Captain Lewis said. "We must find the Shoshones. I will take three men and look for them."

Sacajawea heard the horses first. Then Captain Clark heard them, too. "My people!" she said. "My people are near."

Sacajawea walked with Captain Clark through the Shoshone

camp. She looked from face to face. She did not see her mother, her sister, or her brother. They were not here.

"Come," said Captain Clark. "We will need you to speak for us, Sacajawea."

Sadly she followed the Captains into a tall tepee and to the Shoshone Chief waiting inside.

"Cameahwait!" she cried. "My brother. I have found you." Sacajawea threw her arms around the young Shoshone chief.

Cameahwait could not believe what was happening!

Sacajawea's eyes filled with tears as they talked. Her mother and sister were dead. And for all these years, Cameahwait had thought she was dead, too.

Cameahwait stared at the white men and their guns. He had never seen white men before. Sacajawea told him how Captain Clark had saved her life. He was her friend.

"Why do the white men come to the Indians' lands?" he asked.

"They need horses to cross the mountains," she replied. "They are looking for a great water, greater than any river."

"I have heard of this water," said Cameahwait. "I have never seen it. It is a long way from here."

That night Sacajawea could not sleep. Cameahwait had given the Captains twelve horses. Tomorrow they would leave.

"We need you, Sacajawea," Captain Clark had said. "Will you help us?"

How could she leave her people again?

"My heart is heavy," Cameahwait said, "but I know you must go."

Sacajawea could not speak.

"You will come back," Cameahwait said. "You will tell us about the great water."

Sacajawea left her people. She rode proudly on a fine Shoshone horse. A Shoshone brave led the group into the hills.

Higher and higher they climbed. Snow and wind made each step harder. Trees blocked their way. Sacajawea was not sure they would live to see the great water.

Cold and hungry, through narrow paths, they crossed the Rocky Mountains. Then down, down, down they traveled. They made new boats from trees. They ate fish from the rivers. For three long months, Sacajawea and the white men paddled down the western rivers. Indians along the shore stared at this strange group. But when they saw Sacajawea and Pomp, they let them pass.

Then one rainy November day, the long Columbia River got wider and wider. Suddenly, there in front of them, as far as the eye could see, stretched a huge body of blue water.

"The ocean!" the men shouted. "We have reached the Pacific Ocean!"

Sacajawea remembered her brother's words. "You will come back. You will tell us about the great water."

That winter they built a fort near the Pacific Ocean. Their red, white, and blue banner waved in the salty air. Everyone was tired but happy.

"We have done what we set out to do!" Captain Clark said.

Sacajawea was proud that she and her people had helped. She looked out at the ocean. She thought to herself, "I have seen sights I will remember all my life. And I found my people again. I am happy."

When spring came, Sacajawea and the others traveled back up the rivers and over the mountains. Sadly, Sacajawea did not find Cameahwait that spring. We do not know if she ever did. She and Charbonneau returned to the Mandan village.

Sacajawea was the first woman to cross the Rocky Mountains. With Lewis and Clark, she had helped to open the way west. She did not know that she always would be remembered for these things.

Elizabeth Blackwell

Six-year-old Elizabeth Blackwell sat on the dark, well-polished stairs. Peeking between the stair railings, she could see down into the brightly lit parlor. Mama sat in a dainty lady's chair, mending the lace trim on a shawl.

Papa Blackwell stood at the fireplace, warming his hands. Elizabeth thought he looked very handsome in his elegant white suit. Mr. Blackwell wore a white suit to business, no matter what season it was. He was the owner of a sugar refinery, and his white suit stood for the clean, pure white sugar produced by his company.

The only times Mr. Blackwell wore a dark suit were to attend church on Sunday, and when he went to parties or political meetings. Then, like other proper Englishmen of the 1820s, he wore a black wool coat, dark-gray trousers, and a gray-and-black striped tie. Elizabeth thought he looked important in his dark clothes, but she liked his everyday white suits even more.

From where she sat on the stairs, Elizabeth could not see her Aunt Barbara, but she could hear her voice quite clearly. As usual, Aunt Barbara was complaining about Elizabeth. "She can be a most difficult child," Barbara Blackwell said. "Anna and Marianne are such polite little ladies. They are always good and do as they are told. In my opinion, Elizabeth is far too strong-willed and independent for a girl. It's a pity she wasn't born a boy!"

"To my mind," said Mr. Blackwell, "those are fine qualities for a girl. I think no less of my daughters than I do of my baby son, Sam. And if God blesses us with more children, it is the same to me if they are boys or girls."

Barbara sighed heavily. "Your feelings are noble, Brother Samuel, but I fear the results," she said. "What possible use can young ladies make of Latin, Greek, history, and mathematics? A lady need know only a bit of art and music, embroidery, some French, and how to conduct herself properly."

"You must be fair, Barbara," said Mrs. Blackwell in her soft voice. "Anna and Marianne, as you said yourself, are very good little girls. As for Elizabeth, she has a special spark. I am sure she will do great things."

Great things, Elizabeth repeated to herself on the stairs. *Oh, indeed I shall.* And in her mind the six-year-old pictured herself on a big, white horse, leading an army into battle, and then as the captain of a tall-masted ship, sailing into a storm-tossed sea. Then she imagined herself putting the last strokes of paint onto a huge canvas, while a crowd of people cheered the great artist. Then she saw herself healing hundreds of sad, sick children, making those sad faces smile brightly.

"Doctor Blackwell," she said aloud. "That sounds *so* good." Elizabeth yawned, then she got up and tiptoed back to her room. A few moments later she was in bed and fast asleep.

Though she did not know it, Elizabeth Blackwell, born on February 3, 1821, was being raised in a most unusual way. At that time in Bristol, England, where the Blackwells lived, girls were given very little education. Most people felt that girls were not as smart as boys, not as important, and not able to do most things as well as boys.

Women were not allowed to become doctors, lawyers, bankers, or to hold any other important position. They could work as house servants, in factories, in taverns, or on farms, but every penny they earned became the property of their fathers or husbands or brothers. Unless they were very poor, women were expected to stay home and be "ladies."

Samuel Blackwell did not think the way other people did. He believed that there was no such thing as "man's work." He felt that women were as smart and able as men, and that little girls should be as well educated as little boys.

Samuel Blackwell was different in other ways, too. Many well-to-do-English people ignored the injustices of the world, but not Samuel Blackwell. He fought against the slave trade that sent black people from Africa to the United States and the British colonies. He was against child labor, which put five- and six -year-olds to work in the coal mines and cloth mills. He was against wages so low that workers and their families starved to death on them. And he made these feelings very clear to all of his children.

Elizabeth's father was a kind, fair, and loving man. Although in those days a naughty child was usually whipped or beaten, locked up in a room with no food, and punished in other ways, he never spanked his children. Most people believed that harshness was the only way to "drive the devil" out of children who misbehaved, but Mr. Blackwell thought this was a horrible attitude. Not only did he not punish his children, he could even say "no" to them in a loving way.

One time, the girls wanted to climb out an upstairs window of their house and sit on a small, slanted roof. There, they would be able to see all of Bristol and even some of the far-off countryside through Anna's small telescope. But first they had to get permission from their father.

"I will ask Papa," said Elizabeth, who was nicknamed "Bessie."

"No, let me," said Marianne. Marianne's nickname was "Polly."

"I am the oldest," said Anna. "We shall make up a proper request in writing, and I shall take it to Papa."

Anna had the neatest handwriting, and she was the best writer. So Polly and Bessie voted to go along with her decision. Soon the note was written and handed to Mr. Blackwell. His answer, given to the girls that night, was a poem.

> Anna, Bessie, and Polly,
> Your request is mere folly,
> The roof is too high
> For those who can't fly.
> If I let you go there,
> I suppose your next prayer
> will be for a hop
> To the chimney top!
> So I charge you, three misses,
> Not to show your faces
> On parapet wall
> Or chimney so tall,
> But to keep on the earth,
> The place of your birth.

And that, with a laugh, was the last word on the subject. But it wasn't the end of poetic answers in the Blackwell house. Another time, young Cousin Maria came to spend a few weeks with the Blackwells. The guest room, where she slept, was large and very dark and had a large four-poster bed. Maria was scared to sleep in this strange, big room. So, each night Anna and Polly took turns sleeping with her. Elizabeth wanted to take a turn, too. But her sisters said she was "too little."

"The bed is so big," said Elizabeth, offering a solution to the problem, "that all four of us can sleep in it."

"Oh, what a fine idea," squealed Maria.

The girls all agreed, and they wrote a note to Mr. Blackwell, asking permission.

His answer was another poem:

> If you four girls were together to lie
> I fear you'd resemble the pigs in their sty!
> Such groaning!! Such gruntings!!!
> Such sprawling about!!!!
> I could not allow such confusion and rout!!!!!
> So this is my judgment: 'Tis wisdom you'll own
> *Two* beds for *four* girls are far better than one!

There was a lot of love and happiness in the home of Samuel Blackwell. But there was sadness, as well. Mr. and Mrs. Blackwell always wanted a large family, and almost every year Mrs. Blackwell gave birth to a baby. As often as not, however, the baby did not live. Before little Sam was born, there had been two other baby boys in the Blackwell family. Both had died before they reached two months of age.

It was even worse in other families. Elizabeth had one aunt who gave birth to eight boys and lost all eight of them. It did not matter whether a family was rich or poor. There were not many doctors, and there were no medicines and no cures for most sicknesses.

Every time a baby died in her family, Elizabeth felt the house fill with unhappiness. Her mother would be gloomy for weeks, and her father would sit and sigh with deep sadness. Elizabeth, who was very close to her father, felt terrible. "Papa, why doesn't anybody help babies to live?" she asked him one day. "Why isn't there someone to take care of all the sick people? It's wrong, the way things are."

"Yes, Bessie," he said, stroking her hair gently. "There are

many things wrong with this world, and we must do everything in
our power to set them right."

Elizabeth's mouth set in a hard, straight line. "When I grow
up, I shall be a doctor," she said. "I shall help babies to live and
children to stay healthy and—"

"—and if anyone can do it," Mr. Blackwell said, picking up her
sentence, "you can. You are a very clever and good little lady. If
you study hard and really believe you can do it, nothing can stop
you."

That night, as eight-year-old Elizabeth lay in her bed, she
thought, "Papa says I can be anything I want, and he is a very
smart man. So he must be right!"

Elizabeth *did* study hard. There were many books in the
house, and she read every one. Each year, at Christmas, the
Blackwell children put together a small book of their own poems
and stories. This would be their present for Mr. Blackwell. It was
always easy to tell which ones his Bessie had written. They were
very serious and done in carefully printed letters. Like everything
else Elizabeth did, her papers had to be just right—no matter how
long it took!

At lessons with Eliza Major, the children's governess,
Elizabeth was always the best pupil. The others might want to run
outside and play before "school-time" was over, but never
Elizabeth. She wanted Miss Major to give her more and more
work. She was the same with all the tutors who gave lessons to the
Blackwell children. Elizabeth was never bored with learning and
doing new things.

None of the children went to a school. Instead, they learned
from the tutors who came to the house. There were no schools in
England where girls could study serious subjects. Being tutored
was the only way for them to be educated. There were good
schools for boys in Bristol, but these schools were only for
members of the Church of England. The Blackwells were members

of the Independent Church, a religious group like the Quakers. Because of their religious beliefs, the Blackwell boys could not attend the better schools in Bristol.

In those days, boys and girls did not have classes together—or even spend much time together, but since there were no schools for them, the Blackwell children did most things together. This was the normal way of life for their family. The boys and girls were treated equally at lessons, at play, at the dinner table—in just about every way possible.

Years later, when Elizabeth was a medical student, she would remember the boy-girl equality at home. When her classmates—all young men—teased her, she just laughed it off. They might have felt strange to be in a class with a young woman, but Elizabeth was used to having boys as classmates. Often, their teasing reminded her of her brothers.

For a long time, Mr. Blackwell's sugar business was very successful, and the family lived quite well. There was plenty of money for the big house in Bristol and the summer house in the country, for servants and for tutors, and to support Mr. Blackwell's four sisters who lived with them, and every other friend or relation who needed money.

Then, at the beginning of 1832, things changed. The sugar plant started losing money, and Mr. Blackwell lost even more money in bad investments. Suddenly, the family was not rich. Mr. Blackwell made a decision. "We are going to America," he announced one evening.

"Why must we leave England?" asked young Sam.

"For many reasons," said Mr. Blackwell. "There, you will be able to go to school. That is something you cannot do here. And America is a land of freedom, new ideas, opportunity for all." He seemed to look right at Elizabeth as he spoke.

Mr. Blackwell went on, giving more reasons, and explaining his feelings. Then he asked everyone how they felt about the move.

When all the talking was done, only Aunt Ann refused to go. The others immediately began making plans for the start of a new life in the New World.

Once the decision was made, nothing could change Mr. Blackwell's mind, not even a group of Bristol merchants begging him to stay. They offered to lend him any amount of money he needed, and, they said, he could pay it back whenever he wanted to. Mr. Blackwell was very grateful for this kind offer. Even so, he told the merchants, the Blackwells were leaving for America that summer.

On a bright August morning in 1832, the *Cosmo,* her sails billowing in the wind, left England with the Blackwells aboard. The seven weeks and four days that followed were a living nightmare. More than two hundred people were crowded aboard the ship. Most of them were steerage passengers—packed like cattle in the filthy, rat-infested blackness far below decks. Even for first-class passengers, like the Blackwells, the trip was miserable. Six or more people were crammed into each "good" cabin. The portholes leaked, water soaked everything, and chill winds blew through the cabins day and night.

Elizabeth was seasick for much of the voyage, but that was nothing compared to the suffering of many others aboard the *Cosmo*. Below decks, there was an outbreak of cholera. This disease, caused by unsanitary living conditions, claimed many lives among the steerage passengers.

During the final days of the voyage, Elizabeth was strangely quiet. She would stand on deck, staring out over the water. One day, her father said, "Are you homesick, Bessie? Are you afraid of what lies ahead in America?"

Elizabeth shook her head. "No, I am sad about what is happening on this ship," she said. "Yesterday I heard Captain Gillespie say that it was a good crossing. He thinks it good because not everyone in steerage has cholera, and that more than half of them are still alive. How can that be good? I think it is the most frightful thing I have ever heard."

"But there is cholera on every ocean voyage," Mr. Blackwell said.

"Why *must* it be that way?" Elizabeth demanded. "Why *must* we think all those deaths are normal? It's wrong, Papa! I think we have to prevent diseases, like cholera and smallpox and the others. There have to be doctors who show people how to stay well, and to help them when they do get sick. That is what I want to do when I am older!"

Soon after the *Cosmo* reached the United States in October 1832, the Blackwells settled into a house in New York City. Not long after that, Mr. Blackwell became deeply involved in anti-slavery activities. Many meetings were held in the Blackwell house. Elizabeth met William Lloyd Garrison, the editor of the *Liberator,* a newspaper devoted to ending slavery. Other visitors she came to know were Dr. Lyman Beecher, the famous minister, and his daughter, Harriet Beecher Stowe, who would one day write *Uncle Tom's Cabin.* She also met Horace Mann, the great educator, and Ralph Waldo Emerson, the noted writer.

The 12-year-old girl was getting a rare education just by living in that house. The visitors she spoke with included many of America's finest thinkers. Their words and deeds would change the country. These were the people who organized the underground railroad, which was used to smuggle slaves to safety, and who fought against child labor and the unfair treatment of women.

As she listened to these people, Elizabeth's faith in herself grew stronger. She needed this faith. No medical school had ever accepted a female student. In fact, women were not welcome at *any* college. But Elizabeth had her mind set on changing this. No matter how long it took or how hard she had to work, she was going to become a doctor.

The next five years were busy ones for Elizabeth. When she wasn't in high school herself, she was helping her sisters Anna and Marianne to teach others. The three sisters had set up a small school for African-American children, who could not get an education any other way. Then several of her brothers and sisters fell ill with a severe fever, and Elizabeth nursed them back to health.

At first, Mr. Blackwell's sugar business did well in New York, but after a while it began to lose money. The problems came one after another. A fire raged through his sugar refinery, destroying everything but the four walls, then a bank failure wiped out most of Mr. Blackwell's savings. And through it all his health began to fail.

Because he hoped things would be better in a new place, Mr. Blackwell moved the family to Cincinnati, Ohio. There, he planned to start the first sugar refinery west of the Allegheny Mountains, and he hoped that his health would improve, too. But it was not to be. Soon after the family arrived in Cincinnati, Mr. Blackwell's illness worsened, and within a few months he was dead.

Mrs. Blackwell, left with nine children and no money, showed great strength. She called the family together and said, "We shall start a small school. Anna, Marianne, and Elizabeth will be its teachers. Samuel and Henry will go to all the houses and tell people of the school. Emily, Ellen, Howard, and George will be good children, and help in any way they can."

Running the school was hard work, but it paid for their food and housing. Elizabeth put in long hours of teaching, even though she was impatient to get on with her plans for the future. She devoted every free moment to her own studies. Since her father's death, she had become even more serious about medicine. Now the teenager began reading and learning from every medical book she could find. She asked questions of any doctor willing to speak with a woman about medicine, but even those who answered her questions tried to discourage her from trying to become a doctor.

"No medical school on earth will have you," said one doctor. "It is ridiculous...unthinkable...impossible!"

Elizabeth did not give up. She wrote a letter to Dr. Abraham Cox, who had been the Blackwell's family physician in New York. He was the first doctor to encourage her, and he sent her the names of medical schools and told her how to apply to them. But he too warned her not to raise her hopes very high.

For the next few years Elizabeth continued to teach and study books about medicine. At the same time, she applied to one medical school after another. Not one would accept her. Then, in October of 1847, she received a letter of acceptance from Geneva Medical College in New York State. She was overjoyed. In almost no time her bags were packed, and she was on a train heading for school.

It was only when she arrived there that Elizabeth learned the hardest months and years were still to come. There were teachers who hated her, and teachers who would not let her into their classrooms. Fellow students mocked her, insulted her, even threatened her. More determined than ever, she completed her studies and graduated with high honors. She was, at last, the first woman doctor in the world!

In the years that followed, Dr. Elizabeth Blackwell blazed new trails in medicine. In addition to setting an example for other women seeking careers in medicine, she established a hospital and clinic called the New York Infirmary for Women and Children. She also founded a medical school for women, helped to train nurses for duty in the Civil War, and wrote many books on health and the prevention of disease.

Not only was Elizabeth Blackwell the first woman doctor, she was also first in many other ways. Long before most other doctors saw the importance of cleanliness and proper diet, Dr. Blackwell was showing people why these things were so important. She called it "preventive medicine," saying that "even better than curing ills is seeing that ills do not happen in the first place."

Elizabeth Blackwell never forgot all the needless infant deaths she had seen when she was a girl—or the cholera epidemic aboard the ship that brought her to America. She gave her whole life to fighting ignorance and illness. When she died in 1910, at the age of 89, Dr. Elizabeth Blackwell had written a shining chapter in the history of medicine—and humanity.

Clara Barton

Christmas was always a happy time in the Barton house, but December 25, 1821 was an especially wonderful day. That was because this bright Christmas morning saw the birth of a healthy baby girl to Sarah and Stephen Barton.

The infant was washed and wrapped in a warm blanket. Then Captain Barton called his four other children into the bedroom to see their newborn sister. Seventeen-year-old Dorothy hurried in. She leaned over the cradle and smiled. Stephen, fifteen years old, and David, thirteen, joined her. Then in marched ten-year-old Sally, delighted not to be the family baby anymore.

Clarissa Harlowe Barton, the newborn's full name, brought endless joy to everyone. She was a sweet, calm baby who almost never cried. She was also a very smart little girl. This pleased her brothers and sisters. Baby Clara was their pet, and they gave her lots of love and attention.

Dorothy, a teacher at a local school, started her baby sister on the ABC's when she was only two years old. Clara was a good pupil, and she was reading by the time she was three. Sally did her share, too, teaching Clara to spell and to write. Stephen taught his little sister arithmetic. Before she even started school,

Clara could do simple addition, subtraction, multiplication, and division.

David taught her something very different. As Clara wrote years later, "He was the Buffalo Bill of the surrounding country. . . . It was David's delight to . . . throw me upon the back of one colt, and spring upon another himself. Then he bid me to cling fast to the mane, and we galloped away . . . They were merry rides we took."

Clara was also her father's little pupil. He would sit her on his knee and tell her all about his battles as a soldier in the Indian Wars. Together, they studied maps, tracing the battle lines of the army's fierce encounter with the great warrior chief, Tecumseh. Mr. Barton taught Clara all of the military ranks, from private through general.

Only Mrs. Barton did not play teacher. "My mother," Clara remembered, "like the sensible woman that she was, seemed to conclude that there were plenty of instructors without her. She attempted very little . . . and looked on the whole thing with a kind of amused curiosity to see what they would make of me. Indeed, I heard her remark many years after that I came out of it with a more level head than she would have thought possible."

Even Button, the family dog, took special care of Clara. From the moment she was born, she was followed around by the white-haired, black-eyed animal. If Clara fell, Button tried to pick her up. If she dirtied her face and hands, he licked them clean. Every day, wherever she went, he trailed. Then, at night, when Clara knelt by her bed to say her prayers, Button sat beside her. When she got into bed, Button would jump onto the covers and curl up at her feet. There he stayed until morning, her protector and friend.

Except for Sundays at church, Clara's first years were spent at home with her family. She had no other children to play with. Still, she wasn't unhappy. She had books to read, lessons to learn, horses to ride, and fields to run in with Button. Best of all, there were the six big people who loved her so much.

Then, when she was four, Stephen lifted her onto his shoulders and carried her through the snowdrifts to Colonel Richard Stone's school. It was the first day of winter term, and Clara's first day at school. In the early 1800s, school was made up of two terms, each lasting three months. There was a winter term and a summer term. Most youngsters had to help with the planting in the spring and the harvesting in the fall, so they didn't go to school then. Only the youngest pupils went to school in spring and fall.

Stephen kissed and hugged Clara, and said, "Be a good girl. I'll see you when school lets out." And he left.

Clara didn't know any of the other children, and she didn't know how to make friends. She was also much younger and smaller than any of the others. Some of the students—the ones who sat in the big seats in back—were teenagers. Even among the younger children, there was nobody younger than six years old. For the first time in her life, Clara felt scared and alone.

Colonel Stone rapped for attention on his desk. All talking stopped. He gave the bigger students arithmetic problems to do on their slates. Then he called the little ones to his desk. Holding up a spelling book with the alphabet in it, he began to point out the letters. As he said them out loud, Clara said them along with him.

"I named them all," Clara wrote years later. "Then I was asked to spell some little words, 'dog,' 'cat,' and so on."

Clara spelled them all correctly. Then she politely told Colonel Stone that she could spell even harder words. He tested her, and Clara did very well. Colonel Stone told her to sit with the bigger children. Clara was proud to be with the better readers. She had no trouble keeping up with them, but she continued to be lonely. When it was play-time, the big children paid no attention to her, and the little children, not knowing how to act with this different girl, did not welcome her into their group.

Clara put every bit of her energy into learning. Geography became her new favorite subject when Colonel Stone gave her an atlas. She kept it with her day and night, reading it every chance she got. Clara's interest in geography would be very important to her when she grew up. Clara always felt travel was easy and natural. She could picture, in her mind, the map of any place she was going to visit. New places never seemed strange to her, even if they were in another country. That was because she knew so many facts about them.

During the Civil War, when she was a battlefield nurse, Clara's knowledge of geography was of great help. She had no trouble reading military maps and memorizing them. She was never afraid of getting lost, and she could find any outpost, no matter where it was. This made it possible for her to bring aid to wounded soldiers quickly. Many lives were saved, thanks to Clara's childhood love of geography.

Life wasn't all school and study for Clara. She was also an active child, ready for any new game or adventure, and her brothers were always ready to take her out to play. One winter Sunday, long before dawn, Clara heard someone whistling under her bedroom window. She looked out, saw Stephen and David, and threw open the window.

"Dress warmly and come down," David whispered. "We're taking you skating."

"But I don't know how," Clara said.

"We'll teach you," Stephen said. "Hurry up. we'll wait here."

Clara rushed to dress and join her brothers, who were going to the ice-covered pond. The boys tied skate runners to her boots and wrapped two long woolen scarves around her waist. They each held the end of a scarf, to keep Clara on her feet.

The twinkling stars began to fade as the sun rose. Clara's

cheerful laughter was like a bell tinkling on the crisp morning air. The boys pulled her back and forth over the smooth ice until one of her skates caught in a crack, throwing Clara to the ice. When she looked at her knees, the right one was bruised and cut a little, but the left one was badly cut and bleeding steadily.

David and Stephen took the scarves off Clara's waist and wrapped them around her knees. Then they helped her back to the house.

"We're sure to be punished for hurting Clara," said David.

"You will not be punished for anything!" Clara told them. "No one will even know that we went skating. I will keep my knees bandaged and my mouth closed."

Clara's long dress hid her injured knees, and she walked very carefully all day long. Even so, her left knee hurt terribly, and it was hard not to limp. But she could not let the pain show. That would give away their secret!

As hard as she tried, it became clear the next day that something was wrong. Clara let her parents look at her right kr and told them, "I tripped on the stairs yesterday."

Mrs. Barton put a proper bandage on the slightly injure knee and told Clara to walk the stairs more slowly.

Now that her parents knew she had a bruised knee, C could limp about the house without fear. But she thoug' funny that nobody noticed that she was limping on the

The left knee, still wrapped in the scarf, soon becan At last, Clara had to show it to her parents. They called doctor, who cleaned the wound and put on a fresh banc Before he left, the doctor told Captain Barton, "That w: case, but she stood it like a soldier." Then he gave Clara rest the leg for three weeks.

To make it easier for Clara to sit still for three long Bartons gave her a copy of *The Arabian Nights*. It was a filled with marvelous stories and beautiful pictures, and (

it. Many years later, she remembered this book as one of her favorites.

But Clara felt very guilty. She could not eat or sleep. She knew she should be punished for hiding the truth about her accident, and for causing her parents such trouble and worry. Finally, her mother, seeing that something was bothering Clara, asked what it was.

Clara confessed all. Then, as she remembered years later, "My mother came to the rescue, telling me soothingly that she did not think it the worst thing that could have been done, and that other little girls had probably done as badly."

Mrs. Barton told Clara how she had misbehaved herself, when she was a child. She had gone riding on an untamed horse, even after her father had forbidden it, and she had been thrown off the horse and hurt. "I did not need to be taught that lesson twice," Mrs. Barton told Clara. "I did not disobey my parents after that. And I think you will learn the same lesson I did."

Mrs. Barton was right. Clara had learned her lesson. She also learned how it felt to be in pain and need medical care. She thought of this many times when she was an adult. As Nurse Barton and founder of the American Red Cross, she made the easing of pain and suffering her life's work.

In the winter of 1829, when Clara was eight, she went away to boarding school in a nearby town. It was a high school, also run Colonel Stone, and it was one of the best schools in that part of Massachusetts.

Clara's parents had two reasons for sending her to boarding 1. It would give the extremely bright youngster the chance to Latin, ancient history, and many other new subjects. They pped that living in a house with other children would help rcome her great shyness.

ra loved the schoolwork, and was one of Colonel Stone's ents, but being away from home didn't cure her shyness. It just made her homesick. She cried all the time, did not want to eat, and had little to do with the other children. Clara had been there only one term when her father, Colonel Stone, and the Barton family doctor all agreed that she would be better off at home.

Her education did not stop. Once more, her brothers and sisters took over the job of teaching her. Clara learned a lot more on her own as well. Early in 1830, the family moved into an old house that needed a great deal of work. Sylvanus Harris, a local painter and paperhanger, was hired to do the job. Clara watched him for hours, mixing colors, painting, and making his own putty and plaster.

Mr. Harris's work was so interesting that Clara wanted to try it, too. So, in a timid voice, she asked him, "Will you teach me to paint, sir?"

"With pleasure, little lady," he said. "If your mamma is willing, I should very much like your help."

Mrs. Barton gave her permission. The next morning, dressed in an old smock, the little girl reported to Mr. Harris. "I was taught how to hold my brushes," Clara wrote, "to take care of them, allowed to mix and blend my paints, and shown how to make putty and use it."

Clara worked with Mr. Harris day after day. She enjoyed every minute of it, and when the work was done after a month, she was very proud of herself and pleased to have learned so much. But she was also sad that there was no more to do.

The last night of Mr. Harris's job, when Clara went to her room, she found a box on her candle stand. In it was a tiny locket, engraved with the words: "To a Faithful Worker." Clara kept that locket all her life.

She also kept the skills she had gained. As an adult, she did her own painting and wallpapering wherever she lived. As she liked to point out, "People should not say that this or that is not worth learning, giving as their reason that it will not be put to use. They can no more know what information they will need in the future than they will know the weather two hundred years from today."

When she was 11, Clara had to take time off from her schoolwork. Her brother David had been seriously hurt falling off a barn roof. It took two years for him to recover, and Clara was his devoted nurse for all that time.

Once David was on his feet again, he taught Clara a number of skills he felt were important. She learned to drive a nail properly and to use a hammer and saw. She learned to throw a ball far and accurately and to tie sturdy square knots. Most important, David taught her how to plan her work carefully, and how to do a good job from start to finish. Clara, as always, was an "A" student.

As soon as David was completely recovered, Clara returned to school where she studied grammar, English literature, composition, history, philosophy, chemistry, and writing. Her parents were pleased with her high grades, but worried that she was still terribly shy. They wondered what her future would be if she stayed this way.

When Clara was 15, a guest at the Barton home made an interesting prediction about her future. He was L. N. Fowler, an expert in the field of phrenology. Phrenology was a popular "science" of the time. Phrenologists believed there were 37 small sections in the human head. Each of these sections controlled some aspect of a person. There were sections for size, weight, hope, humor, secretiveness, and so on. Phrenologists also believed they could "read" a person's character by reading the bumps on the head.

Mr. Fowler felt Clara's head and said, "The sensitive nature will always remain. She will never assert herself for herself. But for others she will be perfectly fearless. Throw responsibility upon her. She has all the qualities of a teacher. As soon as her age will permit, give her a school to teach."

Perhaps after hearing Mr. Fowler's words, Clara began to gain courage and faith in herself. If he said she had the strength to be a teacher, why then, that's just what she would be! So the girl who was too shy to speak up when she was a student, became a teacher in charge of 40 children. She was only 17. Some of her students were almost as old as she, and a few were bigger than their small, slim teacher, but that didn't scare her.

The biggest pupils were four teenage boys. Clara was warned that they had bullied last year's teacher. On her first day as their teacher, she set out to prove that she was in charge. All morning Clara kept firm control of the class, while the teenage boys watched her for signs of weakness. Then came recess.

Outside, the class began to play ball. Clara asked if she could get in the game. This was just the kind of thing the four boys were waiting for. Now they'd make her look foolish in front of everybody.

But Clara—who had learned to play ball well at home—surprised them. Very quickly, the boys saw that Clara was a fine athlete. She was strong and could run fast. She could throw a ball as straight and as far as any of them. They soon had a deep respect for their young teacher.

Clara never had a bit of trouble from those boys—or anyone else—at the school. Her career as a teacher continued until 1853. During that time, she taught at several schools in Massachusetts and New Jersey. Then, in 1854, she moved to Washington, D.C., where she became the first female clerk in the United States Patent Office. But it wasn't until the bloody Civil War began that Clara Barton began her greatest service. Learning of the needs of the soldiers, she plunged herself into serving those needs. She had no title or help from the government. She was simply doing what she felt was right.

From the start, no task was too hard for Clara to undertake. Still too shy to speak up for herself, she made speeches to large groups, begging for money to buy bandages, medicine, food, clothing, soap, towels—anything and everything the soldiers needed. As the war went on, Clara Barton became a living legend. She was called the "Angel of the Battlefield," nursing Union and Confederate soldiers with equal love and attention.

After the Civil War ended, Clara traveled to Europe. There, she was honored by many governments for her bravery and goodness. It was there that she learned of a new organization called the Red Cross. The aim of the Red Cross was to help people in need, in war and peace. Its flag—a red cross on a field of white—told everyone that help was at hand.

Clara returned to the United States, determined to make the Red Cross a symbol of help and mercy throughout her own nation. She spent the rest of her long life doing just that, bringing aid wherever fire, flood, or any other form of disaster struck. When Clara Barton died at the age of 90, the Red Cross had become a permanent part of American life.

Helen Keller

The sweet scent of honeysuckle floated through the air. The sun was warm. A chickadee hopped along a tree branch, singing. A golden-haired baby, just one year old, sat on a blanket in the grass and looked up at the bird. She laughed at its merry, piping song. Then she looked down at the doll in her lap. She liked its orange woolen hair and button eyes.

"Helen, come to Mama, darling."

The little girl turned around. She saw her mother standing nearby, arms outstretched.

"Ma-ma. Ma-ma," said the child. A smile shining on her face, little Helen stood and toddled to her mother's arms.

"Happy birthday!" said Mrs. Keller. "One year old today! Come in and see the presents everyone has brought for you."

The presents looked pretty in their shiny wrappings, but Helen had eyes for just one thing: the birthday cake. It had white icing and pink sugar roses with mint-green leaves. Best of all, it had one tiny candle glowing on top. The flame danced and fluttered while the little girl giggled with delight.

Helen Keller would never see another birthday candle or ever again hear her family sing "Happy Birthday" to her. For when she was one-and-a-half years old, she suffered a terrible sickness. Her fever raged for days, and doctors could do nothing to help her. It was the winter of 1882, and doctors didn't know many things they know now. They did not have the medicines that are used today to treat many illnesses. The only thing they could do for Helen was to make her comfortable and pray for her recovery.

Helen did recover, but the illness left her totally blind and deaf. At first, Mr. and Mrs. Keller hoped this nightmare would pass. Mr. Keller would stand near his daughter and clap his hands together sharply, but Helen did not turn toward the sound. Mrs. Keller would hold up an oil lamp, but Helen did not turn toward the light.

Helen's parents finally accepted the sad truth of their daughter's blindness and deafness, but when friends told them that their child was feeble-minded, they could not accept that. They knew that Helen had a bright mind, and they never gave up hope that, one day, she would show the world just how smart she was.

The Kellers did their best to make Helen's life full and happy. They gave her lots of love and attention, letting her roam freely around their home in Tuscumbia, Alabama. She ran through the fields with Belle, the family setter, and rode the small pony that lived in the barn behind the house.

The little girl loved the smell of flowers in the garden, fresh bread baking in the kitchen, and her mother's perfume. She loved the taste of cold ice cream and hot biscuits. And she loved the rough feel of tree bark under her fingertips, and the silkiness of Belle's fur. There were moments of happiness, like tiny islands in a vast ocean. But mostly, Helen's life was like being alone in a silent, dark room. Whatever she felt was locked inside—her love had nowhere to go, her anger had nowhere to go, her fears had nowhere to go.

When Helen was five, Mrs. Keller read about a woman named Laura Bridgman, who was also deaf and blind. She had been taught to read and write, and to "talk" to people by using a finger alphabet. Her teacher was Dr. Samuel Gridley Howe, of the Perkins Institute for the Blind, in Boston, Massachusetts.

Laura Bridgman's story gave the Kellers hope that something could be done for Helen. As soon as they could, they took her to Baltimore, Maryland, to see an eye specialist. The doctor examined Helen, and said, "I'm sorry, her condition will never change. But she can learn a lot of things. There is nothing wrong with her mind. I have a suggestion to make."

"What is that?" Mrs. Keller asked. "We'll do anything that might help Helen."

"I think you should take her to Washington D.C., to see Dr. Bell. He has had great success teaching deaf people."

The Kellers took a train to the nation's capital. There, they went to see Dr. Alexander Graham Bell. Today, Dr. Bell is remembered mainly as the inventor of the telephone, but in those days he was best known for the school he had founded, where teachers were trained to instruct deaf students.

Long train rides, strange hotels, meeting many new people—it all confused and frightened Helen. But Dr. Bell was very gentle. He sat her on his knees and guided her hands to his face. She felt his droopy mustache and heavy beard. Then he held his gold pocket watch against her cheek. She could feel the steady *tick-tock*, and she nodded her head in rhythm with it. Helen was not afraid of this kind man, and she sat still while he examined her. Then he told the Kellers, "I am certain that this clever little girl can be taught to communicate with others."

Dr. Bell suggested that Mr. Keller write to the Perkins Institute, where Laura Bridgman had learned the finger language. Perhaps the director, Michael Anagnos, could find the right teacher for Helen.

Mr. Keller did write the letter and soon received an answer. Mr. Anagnos knew of a young woman who would make a perfect teacher and companion for Helen. Her name was Annie Sullivan. Arrangements were made quickly, and Annie Sullivan arrived in Tuscumbia on March 3, 1887. Mrs. Keller met her at the train, and they rode back to the house in a horse-drawn carriage.

Helen did not know why there was so much excitement in the house, but something told her that today was very special. When she could not find her mother anywhere, Helen went to the front door and waited.

The carriage drew up in front of the house, and Annie Sullivan got her first look at Helen. The young girl's dress was dirty. Her light-brown curls were tangled and uncombed. She stood tense and frightened, like a startled fawn in the forest.

Mr. Keller helped Annie down from the carriage. She began to walk up the wooden steps to the front porch. When Helen felt the vibrations made by the footsteps, she rushed at the stranger. Annie caught her before the wild charge knocked both of them down the steps.

Annie knelt and put her arms around Helen. She smiled as the child's fingers felt her eyes, her nose, her hair, and her hat. When Helen was finished "meeting" the stranger, Annie took her hand and they walked into the house, side by side.

Their first days together were not easy. Annie was unhappy about Helen's wild behavior. The child was allowed to walk around the dining table, sticking her fingers into everybody's food and taking whatever she wanted. She was very rough with Mildred, her baby sister, and with the dog, Belle. Helen would not let anybody comb her hair or wash her face and hands, and she would fly into a fierce rage when anyone tried to make her do something she didn't want to do.

Annie understood why Helen acted this way. Her parents felt so sorry for their unfortunate little girl that they could not bear to punish her, no matter what she did. They never made her obey rules. Annie knew she had to tame this wild young girl. Helen had to learn to get along with other people, for until she did, she could not be taught anything.

First, Annie tried to win Helen's trust. She gave the little girl a doll that had been sent by the children at the Perkins Institute. Helen ran her hands over the doll, smiled, and hugged it tightly. A moment later, Helen felt Annie take hold of her right hand She felt fingers fluttering and tapping on her palm. The tapping stopped. Then again she felt the same tap-flutters on her palm. And again. Helen was puzzled.

Annie was using a special finger language to spell *d-o-l-l* in Helen's hand. She spelled it over and over, but Helen did not understand what was happening. Fear bubbled inside her, and she threw the doll to the floor and rushed from the room.

Later that day, Annie took a piece of cake and touched Helen's hand to it. Helen loved cake and started to grab it. Annie stopped her, and with one hand, she held Helen's left hand so that it just touched the cake. At the same time, she spelled *c-a-k-e* into Helen's right hand. She spelled it again and again.

Helen scowled and started to pull away. Then, suddenly, she stopped. Putting her fingers in Annie's hand, she very slowly spelled *c-a-k-e*. Annie was thrilled with Helen's quick response, and she gave Helen the cake. The young girl ate it happily.

As soon as Helen finished the last crumb, she felt Annie guide her left hand over the doll. Helen wanted it; it felt so soft and cuddly. She tugged at it, but Annie didn't let her have it. Then Helen put her fingers in Annie's hand and spelled *d-o-l*. Annie guided Helen's fingers through the second *l*, then placed the doll in Helen's arms. A smile spread across Helen's face.

This first success filled Annie with joy. Helen could learn! Now there was much to do. They began the next morning. Annie gave Helen milk and spelled *m-i-l-k* at the same time. She spelled *c-a-t*, while Helen petted the purring pet. And in this way, one new word followed another as the day flew by.

Although Annie's pupil showed great promise, there was still the problem of trying to discipline her. Sometimes Helen was very friendly. But at other times she had tantrums. She would kick and punch, shove people or throw things, until she got her way. Annie had to stop that, for she knew that Mr. and Mrs. Keller never would. She asked them to let her have complete control over Helen, and they agreed.

At breakfast the next morning, Annie made Helen sit in her own chair at the table. She would not let the child take food from anyone else. The first time Helen tried to, Annie slapped her hand. Helen pinched Annie, and Annie slapped her hand again. Helen stamped her feet in fury.

Annie dragged Helen to her own chair and made her sit in it. Then she put a spoon in the child's hand and guided it to her food-filled plate. When Helen threw the spoon on the floor, Annie made her pick it up.

Mrs. Keller was crying, and Mr. Keller's face was a mask of pain. They hated to see their Helen suffer so. "She can't help herself," Mrs. Keller said. "She doesn't know better."

"We can help her to know better," Annie said in a gentle voice.

The Kellers left the dining room, and Annie locked the door behind them. Then the battle really began. Annie was determined—Helen would learn to sit in her chair, eat properly, and fold her napkin when she was finished.

Helen walked around, touching every chair. When she found that her parents were gone, she crawled under the table. Annie pulled her out and sat her in her chair. Helen picked up the food with her fingers. Annie wiped them clean and gave her a spoon. Helen tried to drop it, but Annie wouldn't let her. Helen struggled. Annie was stronger.

Helen finally gave in and ate with the spoon. Even so, the battle was not over. When she finished eating, Helen tossed her napkin on the table. Annie made her pick it up, fold it, and place it beside her plate. A moment later, Helen flung the napkin to the floor. Annie made her get out of the chair, pick it up, and fold it again. Helen was sobbing, but she would not give in. Neither would Annie. At last, the napkin remained on the table, folded neatly. Only then did Annie unlock the door and let Helen out.

That night, Annie cried herself to sleep. She hated being harsh with Helen. She really loved the child, and wanted to be her friend, but first, she knew, Helen would have to depend on her. Only then could the real learning begin.

The battle of wills went on, but each day was a bit easier than the day before. One morning, Helen brought her comb to Annie for the first time. The next day, she let Annie get her ready for bed, then tuck her in for the night. And she was learning, too, to sew an apron for her doll, to crochet, to string beads, to "say" new words in finger talk. Annie was delighted. At last, Helen liked her and trusted her. Yet there was something missing. Helen learned to make the words in finger talk, but she didn't *know* that they were words. She didn't know how to use them the way other people did.

Then, one day, Helen and Annie found the key that opened the door to the world for Helen Keller! It was April 5, 1887. Annie described the moment of discovery in a letter to a friend. She wrote: "We went out to the pump house, and I made Helen hold her hands under the spout while I pumped. I spelled *w-a-t-e-r* into her free hand. . . . The word coming so close upon the sensation of cold water rushing over her hand seemed to startle her. She dropped the mug and stood transfixed. A new light came into her face. She spelled *w-a-t-e-r* several times."

Then Helen reached down and touched the ground. Annie spelled *g-r-o-u-n-d* in her hand. Helen looked excited and pointed at Annie. Annie spelled *t-e-a-c-h-e-r*. Helen understood. And from that day on, she always called Annie Sullivan by the name, Teacher.

Now Helen pointed to herself. Annie spelled *H-e-l-e-n K-e-l-l-e-r.* Helen trembled with joy. She had a name, too! Helen grabbed Annie's hand, and they flew into the house together. They found Mrs. Keller. Helen burrowed into her mother's arms, while Annie spelled *m-o-t-h-e-r* on her hand. Helen understood, and she nodded her head. Tears of thankfulness spilled from Mrs. Keller's eyes.

Helen couldn't learn enough to satisfy her thirst for words that day. She moved quickly around the house, touching things, learning the word for each one. Years later, Helen wrote, "It was as if I had come back to life after being dead. . . . Delicious sensations rippled through me, and strange sweet things that were locked up in my heart began to sing."

Helen was up with the sun the next morning, ready to learn more. She woke Annie with a hug and a kiss—and a tug of hands that said, "Hurry! Get up!" It took a while for Helen to get dressed, but not because she made it a battle. As she put on each piece of clothing, she wanted to know all about it. Now she knew she wore a *dress,* and that it had *sleeves,* a *skirt, buttons, buttonholes,* a *collar,* a *belt.*

That was just the beginning. Words poured into Helen. She touched trees and grass and stones, and learned their names. She held an egg in her hand and felt a baby chick break through the shell and hatch. Then Annie's fingers told her all about the miracle of life she had felt.

Her teacher taught Helen to hop and skip and jump, telling her the word for each action. They did the same thing with foods, people's names, animals, flowers, furniture—everything in the world around them.

Annie wanted Helen to feel free and happy, so they spent most of their days outside, doing their lessons under a big tree in the garden. Helen learned geography by making maps with wet dirt. She shaped mountains and valleys, islands and rivers, even whole continents. She learned the shape of the Earth by holding an orange. Annie could hardly keep pace with Helen's endless desire for "more words."

If Helen could read, Annie decided, she would learn much faster, so Annie taught her to read Braille. This is a way of printing words by using raised dots on paper. It was invented by Louis Braille in 1829, so that blind people could read by touch. Annie had Helen feel the braille letter *a* with the fingers of one hand, while *a* was finger-spelled into her other hand. Then *b* and *c*. Helen mastered the braille alphabet right away. Annie brought her books written in braille. Helen loved them so much that she always slept with one in her bed. Next, Annie taught Helen how to write in braille. Before long, Helen was writing stories, notes to Teacher, and letters to the blind children at the Perkins Institute.

Mr. and Mrs. Keller were thrilled at Helen's progress. "You have worked a miracle," Mr. Keller told Annie.

"The miracle is Helen," Annie insisted. "She can learn anything. Why, right now, we are working on ordinary writing. You will soon be reading her letters yourself."

Helen wanted to learn, learn, learn. Annie did her best, but she could see that Helen needed more than she could give her. So, in the spring of 1888, they took a train to Boston. There, at the Perkins Institute, Helen went to a real school for the first time.

Annie sat next to her in every class, spelling out the teacher's words in Helen's hand. Helen learned geography, zoology, Latin, German, arithmetic, English, Greek, and French. She didn't *have* to study all those subjects, she *wanted* to!

From eight o'clock in the morning until six o'clock at night, Helen went to classes. She stopped only for lunch and for an hour of play with other children in the gym. It was very tiring for Annie, who never left her side, but Helen thrived on it.

When Helen was 10, she read about a blind, deaf girl in

Norway who had learned to speak words out loud. Helen wanted
to do the same thing, so Annie took her to the Horace Mann
School for the Deaf in Boston. There, a teacher named Sarah Fuller
began working with Helen. First, Helen placed her hand on Miss
Fuller's mouth and felt the way words are formed. Then Helen
tried to copy this with her mouth.

Helen could not hear her own voice, so she did not know if
her words sounded the way they should. Annie worked with her,
day and night, however, and their reward came when Helen said,
"It is warm," in a clear voice. When they went to Tuscumbia for
summer vacation, Helen's family received a beautiful surprise.

The Kellers were waiting at the train station. Helen, prettier
than ever, stepped down to the platform. Very proudly, she said,
"Mother, I am not dumb now. Mildred, I love you. Father, I am
glad to be home."

This was a moment the Kellers would never forget.

It was a wonderful summer vacation, and when it was over
Helen and Annie returned to school in Boston. This is how they
spent each year as Helen grew into her teens.

One day, Helen told Annie of a new goal she had her heart set
on. She wanted to go to college. Some of her friends felt college
would be too hard for Helen, and that she would be crushed by
failure, but Helen refused to give up her dream.

She studied tirelessly for the entrance examinations. Her hand
printing was slow, so she learned to use a typewriter. She typed her
answers through a nine-hour preliminary exam, plus a full-day final
exam. Helen did brilliantly, winning honors in English and German
and receiving credit in advanced Latin. Now her friends *had* to
believe in her dream!

Helen attended Radcliffe College in the fall of 1900. During
her four years there, she found her life's work: to help others. She
would tell the world her story and show everyone that the deaf and
the blind can learn. Helen wanted to bring hope to the

handicapped. Her life was proof that everyone deserved a chance to learn.

In the years that followed, Helen wrote many books and magazine articles. She traveled around the world, speaking to people of all nations. Until Annie died, in 1936, she was with Helen every step of the way. Polly Thompson, a young Scottish woman, took Annie's place at Helen's side, and together they carried on Helen's work.

During World War II, Helen visited soldiers who had been blinded in battle. She gave them courage and faith in the future. After the war, she worked with blind and deaf children. "I cannot stop to grow old while there is so much work to do," she said, "and so many children to help."

Until her death on June 1, 1968, this most remarkable woman continued to give love, hope, and inspiration to thousands of human beings.

Rosa Parks

It was early in the evening of December 1, 1955 when Rosa Parks finished work at the Montgomery Fair Department Store and caught a bus to go home. She was tired after a long day of sewing in the store's tailor shop.

Mrs. Parks paid her fare, found an empty seat, and sat down. The bus soon filled with passengers, the black people sitting in the back and the white people sitting in the front. In those days, black and white people were often separated that way in the American South. This separation is called racial segregation. It was the law, and in Montgomery, Alabama, this kind of law was strictly enforced.

Rosa Parks sat in the middle of the bus. It was all right for blacks to sit there if no white person had to stand, but on that evening, as the bus filled, a white man was left without a seat. The driver called out to Mrs. Parks and the three other black people in her row to get up and move to the back of the bus. The others followed his orders, but Mrs. Parks stayed in her seat.

The driver stood and walked back to where Mrs. Parks was sitting. "Are you going to stand up?" he asked her.

"No," she said calmly.

"Well, I'm going to have you arrested," the driver said.

"You may do that," Rosa Parks answered.

The driver left the bus and called the police, but Mrs. Parks still didn't move. When two policemen arrived and asked her why she didn't stand, Mrs. Parks responded with a question of her own. "Why do you all push us around?" she asked.

One of the officers answered, "I don't know, but the law is the law and you're under arrest." Mrs. Parks was taken to jail, where she was fingerprinted and put in a cell—all because she refused to give up her seat on a public bus.

Word of Mrs. Parks's arrest spread quickly, and three of her friends soon arrived at the jail to arrange for her release. They were Clifford and Virginia Durr, and Edgar D. Nixon. Mr. and Mrs. Durr were white. He was a lawyer, and they were both active members of the Civil Rights Movement.

E.D. Nixon, a black man, was regional director of the Brotherhood of Sleeping Car Porters, the first black trade union in America. He was also president of the Alabama chapter of the National Association for the Advancement of Colored People (NAACP). Mrs. Parks was also a member of the NAACP, serving as secretary of the Montgomery, Alabama branch.

Mrs. Parks was allowed to leave with Nixon and the Durrs. Raymond Parks had also arrived by then, and he took his wife home. It was dangerous for black people to go against white authority in the South, and he told Mrs. Parks to pay the $14 fine and end the whole matter.

But instead of ending, it was just beginning. When Rosa Parks refused to give up her seat on the bus, she started another American revolution. Mrs. Parks decided it was time to challenge the bus segregation law. She talked it over with Mr. Nixon and the Durrs, and they promised to join in the fight. That night they agreed on what steps to take.

The first big decision was to refuse to pay the fine. It meant that Mrs. Parks might have to go to jail, but she was ready for that. The next step was to organize the whole black community to boycott the city's buses. (A boycott is when people join together and refuse to buy a product or use a service.) The city of Montgomery earned a large amount of money from bus fares, and most of those fares were paid by black people. The boycott's aim was to make the city lose money as long as they kept the bus segregation law.

Late on the night of December 1, a group called the Women's Political Council met and printed a notice that was distributed to blacks all over the city. It read, "This woman's case will come up on Monday, December 5. We are, therefore, asking every Negro to stay off the buses Monday in protest of the arrest and trial. Don't ride the buses to work, to town, to school, or anywhere on Monday. . . . Please, children and grown-ups, don't ride the bus at all on Monday."

Word of the boycott spread during the weekend. Ministers of black churches used their Sunday sermons to talk about the boycott while they praised the courage of Rosa Parks. They told every churchgoer to pass the word to friends, relatives, and neighbors.

The boycott on Monday was a huge success. Hardly any black people took a bus that day, and empty bus followed empty bus all around the city. On that same Monday morning, Rosa Parks appeared in court where she was found guilty of breaking the Montgomery segregation law. She refused to pay the $14 fine, and instead, her lawyer filed an appeal. This meant that the case had to be heard by a higher court. Only the higher court could actually change the segregation law.

When Mrs. Parks and her lawyer left the courtroom, they were stunned to see a crowd of about 500 black people standing silently on the sidewalk and the courthouse steps. When they saw Mrs. Parks, they greeted her with cheers and applause. Mrs. Parks was thrilled, and tears came to her eyes. For the first time in her memory, the black community was openly united. At that moment, Rosa Parks knew she had done the right thing, but she also knew there was a lot more that needed to be done.

That night there was a meeting at the Holt Street Baptist Church. The organizers weren't sure how many people would show up. After all, the black citizens of Montgomery had walked miles that day to support the boycott, and everybody was exhausted. But that didn't stop people from coming.

Minute by minute, the church filled until there were no more seats. Hundreds gathered on the church grounds and in the streets surrounding the building. Loudspeakers had to be set up outside to carry the words of the meeting to everyone.

The big question to be decided at the meeting was, would the boycott continue? The black people were tired, and some were afraid. The white community was angry. Everyone knew what dangers lay ahead—loss of jobs, arrests, violence . . . maybe even death.

Then a new voice spoke up. It was the 26-year-old minister from the Dexter Avenue Baptist church. He had lived in Montgomery less than a year, and most of the people in the city did not know much about him. His name was Martin Luther King, Jr. Reverend King began by speaking about the history of segregation. "There comes a time that people get tired," he said. "We are here this evening to say . . . that we are tired . . . of being kicked about by the brutal feet of oppression."

Reverend King spoke about the dangers of carrying on a boycott. Then he talked about the need for a boycott, and about the rightness of it, warning that there must be no violence on the part of the black community. "The only weapon that we have in our hands this evening is the weapon of protest," he said adding that this "just action" had to lead to freedom.

The crowd hung on Reverend King's every word. When he

inished speaking, there was a vote for continuing the boycott.
Every man, woman, and child roared approval. The boycott went
on!

Rosa Parks became a symbol because of her brave act. In that
way she was special, but in other ways she was a typical black
American. Her history is the story of many black people in the
American South.

Rosa Parks's roots were in Africa. Her ancestors were brought
to America by force, and put to work as slaves. Slavery ended after
the Civil War, but life didn't become much easier for black people.
Rosa Parks was born on February 4, 1913, into a world of
segregation and racism. At the time her family lived in Tuskegee,
Alabama, where her father, James McCauley, worked as a carpenter.
Soon after Rosa was born, the McCauleys moved to nearby
Abbeville, to live with James's family. A few years later Rosa's
parents separated, and Rosa did not see her father again until she
was grown up.

Mrs. McCauley took Rosa and Rosa's baby brother Sylvester
to live with her own parents, in Pine Level, Alabama. Then Mrs.
McCauley, who was a teacher, went back to work to support
herself and her children. Today, a good teacher like Mrs.
McCauley can get a job in any public school, but in those days, a
black teacher could teach only black children in separate black
schools. Black teachers were also paid much less than white
teachers.

There was a great difference between education for blacks
and whites. White schools were well-built, well-equipped, and
the teachers were well-paid. White children had textbooks,
heated classrooms, buses, and a full school year. Black children
went to run-down schools with no heat, no desks, no textbooks,
and no school supplies. They had to walk to school, often many
miles, and they went to school only part of every year. The rest
of the time black children were expected to work in the fields,

picking cotton, weeding, and doing other farm chores.

Although the system was cruel and unfair, black people had no way to change it. The laws made them second-class citizens and kept them that way. Black people who protested or behaved like free human beings were punished. Sometimes the punishment was the loss of a job or land, but often it was much worse.

All over the south there were gangs of white people who used violence to control black people. The worst of these groups was the Ku Klux Klan (KKK). Klan members wore white sheets and hoods to hide their identities. They often committed their terrible deeds at night, burning churches and homes, and killing any blacks they found. Worst of all, they were never punished for any of their crimes.

When Mrs. McCauley went back to teaching, her parents, Rose and Sylvester Edwards, took care of the children. Mr. and Mrs. Edwards owned 18 acres of land where they grew corn, fruit, yams, and many other vegetables. They raised their own pigs, cows, and chickens, and caught fish in a nearby creek. Though the family was poor, there was always enough to eat. Life on the farm for little Rosa and Sylvester was happy and secure, but there was always a cloud that hung over their lives. It was the ever-present danger of the KKK and other racist groups.

One of Rosa's first experiences with racism came when she was five years old. The KKK was very active in her part of Alabama. They rode around at night, destroying black churches, burning crosses on black property, breaking into black homes and killing the people who lived there. Every night, Mr. Edwards sat in his home with a shotgun close by. If the Klan attacked his house, he was ready for them.

"I don't know how long I would last if they came breaking in here," he told Rosa, "but I'm getting the first one who comes through the door."

On those nights Rosa sat on the floor next to her

grandfather's rocking chair. He told her stories about his parents and about his mother's difficult life as a slave. He talked about the Civil War, and what happened when Yankee soldiers came and told the slaves they were free. Rosa loved and admired Grandfather Edwards. He had a very hard life, but he did not let it defeat him. He had an inner strength that was unshakable, and he taught his family not to put up with bad treatment from anyone.

Grandfather Edwards spoke to black and white people with equal dignity and honesty, and everyone knew he expected the same respect from them. It was these qualities that Rosa took for her own. They gave her a solid core of values that stayed with her the rest of her life.

Mrs. McCauley's teaching job kept her away from home all week, but she always spent weekends with her children. During those weekends she taught Rosa and Sylvester to read and write. Even before Rosa started school, she had a strong love of books and learning.

The school Rosa attended had one room for all classes, from first through sixth grade, which was the end of schooling for most black children in Alabama. In the entire state there were only a couple of black junior high and high schools, and they were in the big cities.

When Rosa finished sixth grade she wanted more education. Mrs. McCauley took her daughter to Montgomery. There, the 11-year-old enrolled in the Montgomery Industrial School for girls, better known as Miss White's school. Alice White, who founded the school, came from Massachusetts. She and all her teachers were white, while all the students were black. It was the first time that Rosa was treated as an equal by white people.

Miss White's school was private, which meant the state did not support it in any way. Families who could afford to pay for their daughters' education did so, and the rest of the money to run the school came from local churches and from Mr. Julius Rosenwald, a rich and generous man who believed in education for all people. Mrs. McCauley paid for Rosa's first year at Miss White's school. After that, her daughter was awarded a full scholarship. Rosa studied the usual school subjects, including English, science, arithmetic, and geography. The girls also learned sewing, cooking, and some nursing.

After Rosa had finished eighth grade, Miss White had grown too old to continue working, and the school closed. Rosa stayed in Montgomery and enrolled at Booker T. Washington Junior High School, where she completed the ninth grade. Then she enrolled at the Alabama State Teachers' College for Negroes. At this college, which trained black teachers, the students learned by teaching at a high school run by the college. Rosa attended this high school for the tenth and part of the eleventh grade.

Then Grandmother Edwards got very sick, and Rosa had to leave school to take care of her. After Rosa's grandmother died, the teenager returned to Montgomery and got a job in a shirt factory. This allowed her to earn enough to live on while she went back to school. But then Mrs. McCauley became sick, and Rosa left school again to look after her mother.

Rosa missed school. She wanted to get her high-school diploma and make something of herself, but family responsibilities came first. Rosa's job was to look after her mother and the house. Her brother Sylvester worked as a carpenter and supported the family.

In 1931, Rosa met Raymond Parks. He was a gentle, hard-working barber in Montgomery. They dated for two years and were married in December 1932. Rosa was almost 20 years old, and Raymond was 10 years older.

Parks, as Rosa called her husband, was a fine person in many ways. He encouraged his young wife to finish school, and at home he added to her education by sharing his knowledge and experience. Long before most people heard of civil rights, Raymond Parks was involved in the struggle for equality. He was a member of the NAACP and was glad when his wife wanted to join the group.

Times were hard for most Americans during the 1930s, especially for black people. Those were the years of the Great Depression, when millions of people were out of work. Rosa and Raymond Parks were lucky, for both of them had jobs. They didn't earn much, but they made enough with his barbering and her sewing to pay their bills.

At the end of 1941, the United States entered World War II, and blacks and whites were drafted into the Army to fight for their country. But blacks weren't treated equally, even in the Army. Bigots and racists everywhere felt that liberty and justice were the rights of white people only.

Rosa Parks looked at the segregation all around her and saw clearly that there was no liberty or justice for black people. There was a war to be fought at home too, a peaceful war against injustice. For that reason she became very active in the NAACP.

Rosa Parks led a busy life. During the day, she worked at the Montgomery Fair Department Store. She also earned money doing sewing at home, and as a life-insurance agent. Mrs. Parks's evenings and weekends were often spent working as the secretary of the local NAACP chapter. She kept a record of membership dues, and she wrote letters and information bulletins that were sent around the country to newspapers, radio stations, NAACP contributors, and members. She made sure that instances of discrimination and violence against blacks were recorded. She kept track of legal cases, jailings, lynchings, and other anti-black activities. All of this helped prepare her for her own place in black history. Then came that fateful day in December 1955, and Rosa Parks led the Civil Rights Movement into a new era.

The bus boycott that followed Rosa Parks's brave deed lasted just over a year. On November 13, 1956, the Supreme Court declared the Montgomery bus-segregation laws unconstitutional, and on December 20 the written order from the Supreme Court was received in Montgomery. The next day black people and white people rode the buses together, sitting wherever a seat was available.

The peaceful Montgomery bus boycott set an example that was followed throughout the South. Stores, lunch counters, bus stations, drinking fountains, rest rooms, hospitals . . . one by one, they became equally available to people of all races.

These victories didn't come easily. Churches were bombed, civil rights workers—black and white—were beaten and murdered. Rosa Parks lost her job at the department store and was unable to find work in Alabama. She and her family were threatened regularly. Raymond Parks also was unable to find work, and Mrs. McCauley was ill. Finally, in August 1957, the family left Alabama and moved to Detroit, Michigan. Sylvester McCauley, who had moved there years before, found an apartment for them to live in.

Rosa Parks stayed active in the Civil Rights Movement, and she worked as an assistant to Representative John Conyers of Michigan from 1965 through 1988. Congressman Conyers relied on Mrs. Parks to run his Detroit office while he was away in Washington, D.C.

At the age of 75 Mrs. Parks retired from her government job, but that wasn't the end of her life of service. In 1987, she founded The Rosa and Raymond Parks Institute for Self-Development, the goal of which is to provide education and guidance for young people. Mrs. Parks never forgot the sense of self-worth that molded her life. She wanted to pass on that quality to as many others as possible.

Many honors and words of praise were bestowed upon Rosa

Parks. She was the mother of the Civil Rights Movement, and words cannot do full justice to her accomplishments. But in Montgomery, Alabama, there is a special kind of monument that pleased Mrs. Parks very much. The bus on which she made history ran along Cleveland Avenue. Today, that street is called Rosa Parks Boulevard.

INDEX

American Red Cross, 34, 38

Barton, Clarissa Harlowe (Clara), 29–38
  adolescence, 36, 37
  "Angel of the Battlefield," 37, 38
  childhood, 29–36
  education, 29–32, 34–36
    boarding school, 34
    Colonel Stone's school, 31, 32
    home schooling, 29, 30
  moves to Washington, D.C. 37
  parents, 29, 30, 33, 34, 35
  phrenologist predictions, 36
  Red Cross, 34, 38
  siblings, 29–33, 35
  shyness, 31, 32, 34, 35, 37
  teaching, 36, 37
Barton, David, 29, 30, 32, 33, 36
Barton, Stephen, 29, 31, 32, 33
Beecher, Dr. Lyman, 25
Bell, Alexander Graham, 41
Blackwell, Anna, 17, 18, 20, 26
Blackwell, Elizabeth, 17–28
  childhood, 17–25
  Civil War, 27
  Cosmos, 24, 25
  decides on medical career, 18, 22, 24–26
  education, 22, 23, 25, 27
  medical school, 27
  moves to America, 23, 24
  moves to Cincinnati, 26
  New York Infirmary, 27
  parents, 17–21, 22, 23, 24, 25, 26
  preventive medicine, 28
  religion, 22, 23
  School for African Americans, 26
  unusual upbringing, 17, 18, 22, 23
Blackwell, Marianne, 17, 18, 20, 26
Blackwell, Samuel, 17–26
Braille, 47
Bridgman, Laura, 40, 41